D1539328

TIGER IN CRYSTAL

TIGER IN CRYSTAL

by CRANE JOHNSON
and GERALD BALL

THEATRE PRESS
550 Fifth Avenue
New York 36, N. Y.

TO

FREDA

Library of Congress Catalog Card No. 66-18796

PRINTED IN THE UNITED STATES OF AMERICA BY
Theo. Gaus' Sons, Inc., BROOKLYN 1, N. Y.

TIGER IN CRYSTAL

FREDA
DAVID, her husband
PETER, their foster son
SALLY ⎱
GEORGE ⎰ Peter's friends
JESSICA
LADY DEVENISH
LORD DEVENISH

Setting: The living room of the Brooks home in the suburbs of a city in Scotland

Time: ACT I: An afternoon in early September
ACT II: A few days later
ACT III: A few days later

TIGER IN CRYSTAL

TIGER IN CRYSTAL opened February 1, 1965, at the Pavilion Theatre, Torquay, England, with Michael Hamilton as producer and Gerald Ball as director.

In the cast were:

Patricia Leach as *Freda*
John Cronin as *David*
John Newman as *Peter*
Eileen Sanford as *Sally*
Malcolm McDowell as *George*
Lee Hudson as *Jessica*
Mandy Weet as *Lady Devenish*
Bernard G. High as *Lord Devenish*

Decor was by Dorothy Draper and Jimmy Mooney was Stage Manager.

TIGER IN CRYSTAL
ACT I

*(When the curtains rise it is a late summer afternoon. The
setting is the living room of the Brooks home in Scotland.
Upstage left are stairs leading to sleeping quarters and other
parts of the house. At center back is alcove with French windows. Downstage right is a grand piano and bench. Further
downstage right is an entranceway to foyer leading to house
exterior. A drinks table is against back wall right of French
windows. Near this is door to clothes closet. In the downstage
left area there is a furniture arrangement of settee, low table
and wingback chair. Further downstage left is a doorway leading into hallway and out into the garden area. When the scene
opens DAVID BROOKS is at the piano playing a Haydn
sonata. He is a kindly, distinguished gentleman. He continues
for awhile, then there is the sound of distant happy shouting.
David stops, crosses to the French windows and looks out. He
smiles at what he sees. FREDA enters from doorway left.
She carries a tea set. Freda is a small, nervous, very tense
woman.)*

FREDA: Why did you stop, David. It was lovely.
> *(Freda places the tea set on the table in front of the
> settee)*

DAVID: Come to the window, Freda. Come watch Peter.
> *(At the mention of Peter's name, Freda clutches her
> hands together—a movement she uses throughout the
> play to express her tension)*

DAVID: Peter is on the diving board. I believe he's going
to . . . ah yes, a swan dive. *(Turning to Freda)* Freda, I wish
you could have seen it. Beautifully executed.
> *(Freda crosses slowly to David at window. David takes
> her hand gently and they look out for a brief moment)*

DAVID: *(Looking out)* How good it is to see young people
at play. The beauty of healthy active bodies.
> *(After a moment, Freda turns away from David and
> slowly walks toward the settee)*

FREDA: (*Staring in front of her*) How are we going to tell him, David? How are we going to tell Peter?

DAVID: Sally's on the board now. A jacknife . . . and superbly done. Come, Freda, come to the window and watch the youngsters.

FREDA: If only we had told him years ago. How are we going to tell him. About Jessica. If only we had told him years ago.

(*David crosses over and sits in chair facing Freda*)

DAVID: Supposing we had told Peter. Would that make this moment any easier? These have been happy years. Would they have been happy if we *had* told him?

FREDA: No, perhaps not. But what will happen. What will happen, David, when Peter learns. When he meets her. What will Peter do when he learns about Jessica. What will he do when he sees Jessica?

DAVID: We'll talk with him . . . before Jessica arrives.

FREDA: You must talk with him, David.

DAVID: We'll talk with him together.

(*Freda suddenly throws her face into her hands and sobs. David crosses over and sits beside her on the settee. He lets her cry almost convulsively for a few moments, patting her affectionately*)

FREDA: It's the end of everything.

DAVID: Peter and his friends will be in soon. Dry your eyes, my dear.

FREDA: For fifteen years I've dreaded this day. Fifteen long years. Not a moment has passed without some reminder, some remembrance of the past. The awful past. Not a moment has gone by without some reminder of the future—the dreaded future. For fifteen years, David, I've been living in only the fearful past and the dreaded future. And now today they are one. The past, the future, combined into the terrifying present.

(*David puts Freda's hand in his*)

DAVID: I love you.

FREDA: (*Responding*) Only in your love, David, have I

found sustenance. (*Turning*) These fifteen years. How miserable they must have been.

DAVID: They've been happy years, Freda. Because of you.

FREDA: Because of me. Because of me you were torn away from your home, your friends, your career.

DAVID: My home is here. My friends are here. My career here. Here, Freda, here. With you.

FREDA: I love you, David. I always have. I always will.

DAVID: I know, Freda, I know.

FREDA: How happy—how truly happy these years might have been. If only . . . You are a doctor, David. If only you could take your scapel and cut away memory, cut away guilt . . .

> (*Freda suddenly tears herself away from David and crosses over right to piano*)

FREDA: Fifteen years. Fifteen years!

> (*Freda slips onto piano bench and again places face in hands, but does not cry. David crosses over to piano*)

DAVID: (*Softly*) Don't let Peter and his friends see you this way.

> (*David sits on piano bench besides Freda*)

DAVID: (*Simply*) I love you.

> (*After a moment David continues his playing of Haydn. After a moment, Freda leans over and kisses him, then rises slowly and leans against the piano. David continues playing and reduces his volume when Freda begins to speak. The music continues softly during this next speech by Freda*)

FREDA: Today Peter is to meet Jessica. Poor, poor Jessica. Fifteen years . . . I wonder if she'll be greatly changed. All this time I've tried to imagine how Jessica might be changing. But I can't. She remains the same for me. My sister Jessica. Jessica, Jessica. My sister Jessica. In my memory she is not a woman, but the little girl who held my hand when I was a child. (*Turning to David*) Oh, David, remember—remember. Remember Jessica as a girl . . . Jessica, Jessica. Jessica . . . riding the hounds, jumping the hurdles confidently and beautifully. Jessica dancing by candlelight. Jessica holding all spellbound with her gaiety and charm. Do you remember, David. Do you remember?

DAVID: (*Softly*) I remember. I remember.

FREDA: Fifteen years. Jessica, oh Jessica, how have they changed you?

(*PETER and SALLY enter through hallway down left. They are in their teens. As they are in swimming togs they stand at opening. Both carry towels which they are still using to dry themselves*)

FREDA: (*Almost instinctively*) No, not in the living room. (*Indicates door*)

(*The above speech is almost play-acted by Freda to cover any possible notice of her tear-stained face*)

SALLY: (*Leaving*) Won't be a minute.

(*GEORGE, a youth in his teens, appears at doorway, also in swim togs*)

PETER: Mum, Dad, you remember George Edwards?

FREDA: Of course. We met at the tennis club dance a fortnight ago.

PETER: George has been teaching me how to swan dive.

DAVID: We saw. And very well done I thought.

PETER: Dad, you should let George teach you. Oh, it's a wonderful feeling. To spring off the board high into the air with arms outstretched, gliding like a bird with wings. Then, . . . the clean, piercing descent into the watery depths.

DAVID: I'm afraid my swan dive would end flat on the surface of the water!

PETER: Oh, Dad!

GEORGE: I'd be glad to teach you, Dr. Brooks. Why, last summer in Australia, I saw lots of old people swan diving. Oh, I didn't mean that you . . .

DAVID: (*Good-naturedly*) I'll stick to hitting the wrong notes in Haydn's concertos and leave the diving to you who are younger.

PETER: You know, Dad, it can't be more than a few seconds of time elapsing during the dive, but it seems so long—that moment with arms outstretched, sailing, sailing downward—putting off to the very last moment the necessity of bringing the flight to an end.

DAVID: Like skiing, I imagine.

PETER: In a way, yet different. In that moment, one feels away from earth, away from life. Yet, strangely, at the same time in the closest possible union with life. (*Breaking*) Oh, I *am* becoming philosophical! Is tea ready, Mum?

FREDA: Tea will be ready, Peter, when you are ready—that is, when you've got some clothes on.

GEORGE: (*Turning*) Sally, speed it up in there. I'm freezing.

SALLY: (*Offstage*) I'm hurrying!

PETER: (*To David and Freda*) Has our visitor arrived yet?

(*Freda freezes*)

PETER: (*To George*) Ten days ago Mum and Dad received a letter from France—which I've never been permitted to see—announcing a forthcoming visitor. I know nothing more than that. A most unusual bit of drama in the household of a respectable university professor of medicine! (*To David and Freda*) Come on, tell us, who is the expected guest?

(*Sally appears at doorway dressed in simple dress which she has quickly put on after removal of suit. She wears open sandals and carries swim bag*)

SALLY: I surrender the domain to the men folk.

(*Both Peter and George exit quickly while Sally comes forward into the room*)

FREDA: Tea's ready if you'd like . . .

(*Freda motions Sally to settee and sits at large chair and begins to pour. Sally picks up a piece of bread and butter*)

SALLY: I'm famished! (*Looking at watch*) I promised father I'd be home before three—and it's already after. George has offered to give me a lift and his presence will lessen Daddy's scolding I hope!

(*Freda drops some silver on the plateware. She shrinks back and covers face with one hand*)

13

SALLY: Are you ill, Mrs. Brooks?

(*David attempts to divert attention away from Freda*)

DAVID: (*To Sally*) When does your father return to Parliament?

(*Throughout the next few speeches, David stares with concern in direction of Freda*)

SALLY: In another week. Really, I think his going there is such a waste of time. The party tells him how to vote and he votes. An automaton would be just as effective and less troublesome.

DAVID: Maybe, but perhaps in some odd way your father helps decide *how* the party will tell its members to vote.

SALLY: If there is a way, I'll agree with you it's certainly odd.

FREDA: (*Recovering*) When do you return to University, Sally.

SALLY: Monday. Peter and I thought we'd take the same train.

DAVID: Will you be glad to return.

SALLY: Yes and no. I love being here at home in Scotland. And I also love being in London. I'm happy at both places. I love the lazy, drifting life here and I love the work at University. I confess though that sometimes at University I daydream a bit during lectures. In reviewing my notes in Political Theories, for example, I found little notations on decorating schemes. Ways to decorate my first home. Georgian. Peter agrees.

(*Sally is embarrassed and drops head*)

FREDA: Georgian is lovely. And I've extra pieces.

DAVID: The summer has seemed so short this year. We've hardly seen Peter at all.

SALLY: Perhaps I'm to blame for that, Dr. Brooks.

FREDA: (*Going to Sally*) We are delighted you are with Peter so much, Sally. We're very fond of you, my dear.

SALLY: (*Clasping knees with arms*) You know, I think I must be the happiest girl on earth.

14

FREDA: Hold onto your happiness, Sally. Hold onto it. No matter what happens, don't let it go.

(*Sally looks at Freda strangely. Then the boys reappear with open shirts which they are buttoning. They notice Sally eating*)

PETER: Hey, why didn't you wait for us.

SALLY: Because I'm terribly late and Daddy will be furious. (*Hands George a cup of tea*) Here, drink this and then we've got to leave.

(*George grimaces and begins gulping his tea*)

PETER: This is what I like best about life away from London. The peace, the quiet. Never any rush.

(*Sally frowns at Peter*)

PETER: Yes, it shall be difficult going back. Oh, life may be slow here but not at London University. Why, take tea drinking, for example; never given more than a half hour at a time. Not like here in Scotland.

(*George chokes on his tea*)

GEORGE: You see, you'll have me choking to death—just like poor Mr. Bainbridge.

SALLY: He didn't choke to death, George. He was murdered.

GEORGE: There never was any proof. He could have just choked to death. Drinking his tea.

PETER: What *is* all this . . .

SALLY: Something that happened at Glasgow before you came home.

DAVID: (*Interrupting*) Finish your tea, children.

PETER: What happened?

SALLY: Oh, it's much too sordid.

GEORGE: A man choked to death whilst drinking his tea —and his wife was questioned for days.

SALLY: It was thought she had placed something in the tea to cause a constriction of the throat muscles. Something which left absolutely no trace.

PETER: Almost makes a man fearful of entering marriage, doesn't it.

15

SALLY: (*Toward Peter*) I could never kill a man I had loved. (*To George*) Are you finished, George.

(*Sally rises, takes cup from George and hands it to Peter*)

GEORGE: All my allowance goes on driving silly girls about and I'm treated like somebody's chauffeur.

(*Sally goes to George and slips her hand through his arms*)

SALLY: But such a nice chauffeur. Charming, debonair . . .

GEORGE: (*Embarrassed*) Oh, cut it out . . .

(*Sally has gone to doorway right*)

SALLY: I'm sorry we have to rush away.

PETER: Must you, Sally? (*Crosses toward doorway right*) I had planned to praise your diving to Mum and Dad and I intended you to hear it.

(*Peter kisses Sally gently on the forehead*)

SALLY: Oh, dear. Only the fear of father's Parliamentary tones could tear me away now—But . . . George!

(*The two young people start right saying goodbyes. David crosses behind them*)

DAVID: So, the old people in Australia can swan dive!

(*David puts his arm warmly on George's shoulder and accompanies him out*)

PETER: (*Gaily*) My friends are such nuts!

FREDA: They're perfectly charming, Peter. All of them.

PETER: Now, are you going to tell me about the visitor.

FREDA: (*Evasively*) Have you started your packing, Peter?

PETER: I'll do it Sunday.

(*Peter crosses over to Freda and puts his arms around her*)

PETER: Come on, Mum, tell me. We've always been pals. Never any secrets.

(*Freda escapes reluctantly from Peter kissing him lightly and affectionately*)

FREDA: Nothing needs to be laundered or sent to the cleaners?

16

PETER: I'm a big boy, Mum. I'm just going back to London University. Not to India.

(*Freda crosses over and stands by piano*)

FREDA: (*Softly*) No, not to India. (*Long pause*) How swiftly the years have gone by. Only yesterday you were a little boy. And now you're a young man. Only yesterday a little boy.

PETER: (*Stepping forward*) Aren't you well, Mum?

(*Freda waves hand toward him*)

FREDA: I was just remembering . . . Long ago. Long, long ago. When I was young . . . a little girl. When I was a little girl. When your mother was a little girl. Oh, Peter, if you could only have known your mother as a little girl. She was so good to me, Peter. Your mother was so good to me when I was a little girl.

(*David reenters*)

PETER: Dad, you must tell me about the visitor. I'm only a simple human and I can't stand the suspense any longer.

FREDA: (*Hopefully*) David.

PETER: Ever since the letter arrived, it's been different here. Whenever I walk in unexpectedly you stop talking and change the subject. Twice I've caught the name Jessica. Is that our visitor's name, Jessica? Who is she? Mum? Dad?

(*Freda starts toward stairway up left*)

FREDA: I must change. (*To David*) David, perhaps you'll talk to Peter.

DAVID: Wouldn't it be better for us both . . .

(*Freda almost runs upstairs and off. Peter is amazed*)

PETER: Really, for a respectable doctor's home, this is quite a drama.

(*David walks over and sits in large chair down left. He doesn't speak. Peter crosses over and sits on settee facing David*)

PETER: Something's wrong, isn't it, Dad? What is it? *Is* it because of Jessica? And who is she? *Who is Jessica?*

(*David gets up and walks to bar table near window up stage. He pours himself a drink and turns to Peter*)

DAVID: A drink, Peter?

PETER: (*Surprised*) At this hour!

(*David pours a drink for Peter and brings it to him. Peter just holds it in his hand. David sits again in large chair, takes a drink, pauses a moment, and then looks out*)

DAVID: (*Quietly*) Yes, Peter. It is Jessica. It is Jessica who is coming.

PETER: (*Impatiently*) *Who is Jessica?* And why have I never heard of her?

DAVID: Jessica is someone from the past. From my past. From Freda's past. From your past.

PETER: My past!

DAVID: A most important, a most terrifying part of your past.

PETER: I believe I will have that drink. (*Drinks and then stands*) This explains why you've both been so upset.

DAVID: Sit down, Peter.

(*Peter sits. David rises, takes Peter's glass, goes over to bar table and refills it. He returns and hands glass to Peter*)

PETER: Someone from *my* past! It's all so damned strange.

DAVID: Raising you as our son has been the most important thing in our lives. I think you know that.

(*Peter is embarrassed and nods slowly*)

DAVID: A few moments ago I stood at the window and watched you and your friends at play. At that moment I thanked God for giving me such a wonderful life. Made wonderful by Freda and by you, Peter.

(*Peter stirs a bit in embarrassment*)

DAVID: You are still very young. Those who are young can never really understand those who are older, just as those who are older can never really understand the young. I remember my own father. When I was very young, he could do no wrong. When I was a young man, I thought he could do nothing right. Then I grew older. I no longer judged, but only accepted and

18

tried to understand. Always he was a father, but somewhere in the passage of time he also became a human being. With all the qualities and frailties of human beings. His frailties I overlooked; his qualities I shall never forget. This comes from growing up, Peter. And only from growing up. Becoming older. Becoming old.

(Long pause)

DAVID: *(Turning to Peter)* Peter, we've always led you to believe your parents were dead.

(Peter looks up puzzled)

DAVID: You came to us as a child. When you were old enough to ask questions we told you that your parents had died abroad.

PETER: India.

DAVID: You never questioned further. We never gave you photos. Told you very little of your past.

PETER: *(Soberly)* All I can remember is being here, with you and Mum.

DAVID: Peter, your father *is* dead. He died in France.

PETER: France! But why did you tell me . . . *(Suddenly realizing statement)* You say my father is dead. And my mother . . . my mother?

DAVID: She is alive.

PETER: Alive.

DAVID: Yes. It is she who is arriving this afternoon.

(Peter is speechless)

DAVID: I realize this is a shock to you.

PETER: My mother . . . my mother here this afternoon.

DAVID: She should arrive at any moment.

PETER: Is that why Mum's so upset?

DAVID: Yes.

PETER: The letter . . . the mystery. *(Realizing)* My mother . . . is Jessica!

(David nods)

DAVID: When you are older, Peter, you'll perhaps understand.

19

PETER: Why has she never come here before?

DAVID: I hope, Peter, you'll understand.

PETER: Dad, why has she never come here before?

(*David is silent*)

PETER: Where has she been, Dad? Fifteen years. Where has my mother been?

DAVID: Please, please, Peter, understand . . .

PETER: Where has she been, Dad? Fifteen years. Where has my mother been?

DAVID: (*Simply*) In prison.

PETER: (*Shattered*) Prison!

(*Peter rises and paces about the room*)

PETER: Prison! My mother in prison! (*Sits again on settee and doesn't speak again until after a long pause*) This is the end of everything. Isn't it, Dad? I can't go back to University.

(*David crosses over and stands behind Peter*)

DAVID: Nothing need change. (*Pause*) Forgive us, Peter. Forgive us for not telling you. You are our life, Peter. Forgive us.

(*There is ringing of doorbell. David turns toward doorway right*)

DAVID: That will be her.

(*Peter stands for a moment as if in shock. Freda appears on stairway. Peter turns and goes toward stairway. He almost runs up stairway, but stops at top, turning back*)

PETER: Why . . . was she . . . why was my mother sent to prison?

DAVID: (*After a pause*) The Court found her guilty of murdering your father.

(*Peter stands silently for a moment, then turns and quickly exits. David stands a moment, then crosses towards door*)

FREDA: I can't do it, David, I can't.

(*There is the sound of the doorbell again. Freda turns back*)

DAVID: (*Tenderly*) Freda.

(*David crosses and leads Freda to settee, seats her, and*

then goes to doorway right. He exits and return momentarily with Jessica. JESSICA wears her hair severely parted and tied in a bun. Her face seems to be without make up and she wears a rather severe gray dress. Upon her entrance she stands in room just looking in direction of Freda. Freda grasps her heart area momentarily and rises)

FREDA: Hello, Jessica . . .

(Jessica makes no comment. She stands there a moment, just looking, then she begins walking slowly about the room. Here and there she picks up brightly colored glass objects)

DAVID: It is good to see you again, Jessica.

FREDA: Yes, it's been such a long time.

(Jessica stops momentarily to look coldly at Freda, then slowly continues about the room picking up any brightly-colored object she sees. She sees a small piece of bright blue crystal. She crosses quickly, picks it up and almost runs to the window area, holding it up to the light. She then kisses object, holds it to her breast, and begins to weep silently, fondling and kissing the object. After a moment she begins to walk slowly from window area to downstage area. She seems not to be speaking to anyone in particular)

JESSICA: Do you know what it is like to be without a piece of brightly colored crystal. To have the days, the months, the years drag slowly by without a glimpse of crystal. Is there anything more beautiful than a piece of blue crystal?

(Again Jessica holds the crystal to her breast, drops her head, and weeps softly)

DAVID: Let me get you a drink.

(David crosses to bar table. Jessica slowly lifts her head and looks at Freda)

JESSICA: (*To Freda*) Was this mother's?

(Freda nods. David approaches with a drink but Jessica shakes her head)

21

JESSICA: I remember once . . . long ago . . . seeing a tiger in crystal.

(There is a shudder and a long, looking-out remembrance by Jessica. Then she looks again at crystal in her hand)

JESSICA: Mother loved color, didn't she, Freda?

(Freda nods)

JESSICA: *(Easing herself into large chair facing Freda)* It is strange in prison. Perhaps it is only there that one really discovers oneself. What one cannot live without. *(Silence)* What I missed most besides my son Peter was not freedom, but the loss of color. Isn't that strange? Isn't that silly? Everything in prison was gray or black. It was as if suddenly all color had been drained from the world. Once toward the end of the first year, I found a paper wrapper someone had dropped that had a bit of blue color on it. I seized it and hid it and whenever alone would take it out and look at the blue. But I was discovered and they took the piece of paper away. I knew then that the only way to keep from going mad was to bring color into my escape world—that world each of us created to keep from going mad. For gold I remembered the silk drapes in mother's dressing room. For green, the velvet upholstery in father's den; for yellow, the ribbons I wore on my hair at school; for blue that ocean color of the Italian seacoast; for purple, the lilacs which surrounded our house. I found that only by living in this escape world of color could I endure the world of reality devoid of color. *(Rising)* And when I left prison, they gave me this dress. This gray dress with the vertical cut. Gray for the prison and the vertical cut for the bars of our cells.

(David sits next to Freda)

DAVID: *(Softly)* All this is past. Now there is only the present . . . and the future.

JESSICA: This dress is given to remind women of their gray prison past. Of the gray future women face when finally released from prison. Two things sustained me in prison. My colors. And the memory of Peter. My little boy Peter. Memories of so many things. *(Pause)* Like his toys. Where are they

22

all now? Lost? Abandoned? No. They are here. (*Indicates head*) And here. (*Indicates heart*) Those toys, blue and red, yellow, green, all the colors, those toys of my little boy Peter . . . who is a little boy no longer.

DAVID: Your son is a fine young man, Jessica.

JESSICA: He is here now?

DAVID: Upstairs.

JESSICA: You have told him?

(*David nods*)

JESSICA: (*Softly*) Peter, Peter. (*After pause*) I wonder if it will be possible for me to ever really leave my escape world. That world of color, crystal, and Peter's toys. I wonder if anyone can spend fifteen years in prison and not be driven insane.

DAVID: There will be a period of adjustment, Jessica. We'll work things out.

JESSICA: (*Nodding towards stairway*) When he enters, will he come down those stairs? Will my son Peter come down those stairs to his mother?

(*Both David and Freda nod*)

DAVID: You are to stay here as long as you wish, Jessica. Until you've decided what you want to do.

JESSICA: In the prison we were all taught trades. We had our choice. Factory trades mostly. I chose the garment training.

(*Freda shudders*)

JESSICA: I was taught materials, and cutting, and given a sense of line.

DAVID: There will be no need.

JESSICA: (*Rising*) I was good at it. I was good at it, David. As a girl I designed and now I have been trained. (*Crosses to piano*) I have an uncanny sense of line and an almost unnatural appreciation of color. I have talent and I have been trained. I think this is to be my happiness—my salvation.

DAVID: (*Hopefully*) Designing?

JESSICA: Designing and my son Peter. Perhaps I can open a salon somewhere. And Peter will be with me. Be with his mother. Oh, David, Freda, *this is my dream.* The dream that carried me through that nightmare fifteen years long.

(*At this moment Peter enters the room and starts down the stairway. Jessica freezes and looks at Peter. Peter doesn't look at either David or Freda. He walks slowly toward Jessica, who looks at him, pleading for compassion. When he is near his mother, he stops and looks at her for a moment*)

PETER: (*Softly*) Is it true? Did you . . . murder my father?

JESSICA: (*After a pause*) Yes, it is true.

PETER: But why?

(*Jessica looks at Freda and then turns her face away. Peter looks at Jessica for a moment, torn with emotion, and then runs to right exit. No one on stage moves. After a moment, Jessica looks toward doorway right.*)

JESSICA: (*Softly*) Peter.

(*The curtain slowly closes*)

END OF ACT ONE

TIGER IN CRYSTAL

ACT II

(The setting is the same. It is several days later. Jessica is sitting in the large chair downstage left. She is dressed in her gray prison issued dress and wears her hair still a little severely, but less severe than in Act I. She is knitting something black. Freda sits on the settee facing Jessica. She sits on the edge of the seat, grasping her hands together anxiously. Freda shows the signs of increased strain in her bodily deportment, hair, face and voice. She is under great strain. After the curtains have parted, Jessica continues to knit, but stares at Freda as she does so. Finally, Freda leans further forward on edge of seat as she speaks to Jessica.)

FREDA: Please, Jessica, return my address book to me.
(Jessica continues her knitting)

FREDA: Please, Jessica, return my address book to me.
(Jessica stops a moment, looks at Freda, smiles slightly, then returns to her knitting, still looking at Freda. Freda rises nervously and crosses behind settee)

FREDA: What do you plan to do with it?
(Jessica looks at Freda with the same smile and continues her knitting. Freda crosses around settee and sits down, this time further back into seat. After a moment Jessica speaks)

JESSICA: Lady Devenish is coming at three?
(Freda nods)

JESSICA: She was, I recall, Lord Dunstan's daughter.
(Freda nods)

JESSICA: A very good family. A very influential family.

FREDA: What are you planning to do, Jessica. Why have you forced me to have Lady Devenish here this afternoon?

JESSICA: You will see, my dear Freda, you will see.

FREDA: How am I to explain you to her? What am I to say?

JESSICA: You are to explain nothing. You are to say nothing. You are only to confirm everything I say. Do you understand, Freda, you are to confirm all that I say. You are a woman of standing in the community, your husband highly respected—there will be no reason to doubt your confirmation.

(Freda leans forward again in the settee. At this moment David walks down the stairs, hat in hand. Freda rises)

FREDA: You're not leaving, David?

DAVID: McLeash has run into some problems with the new enrollment procedures, so I'm going down to help him out.

FREDA: *(Anxiously)* Don't go, David. Not just yet. Tea is ready. Stay, David. *(Pleading)* Stay, just for a cup of tea.

DAVID: Well, only for a moment.

FREDA: *(Indicating settee)* Sit there, David. I'll get your tea.

(David crosses over and sits on settee. Freda goes to back of room and pours David a cup of tea)

DAVID: *(To Jessica)* When are your guests arriving?

JESSICA: *(Continuing to knit)* Lady Devenish is expected at three.

(A pause)

DAVID: It has turned into a most pleasant afternoon, hasn't it.

(A pause)

JESSICA: *(Stopping her knitting)* Do you know anything about Peter. Where he is?

(David shakes his head)

JESSICA: *(Coldly)* You should have told him. You should have told Peter. Long ago.

(Long pause)

JESSICA: How is it possible for someone to disappear so completely? *(Pause)* Perhaps he is no longer even alive. *(Pause)* You should have told him, David, you should have told him.

(Freda brings a cup of tea over to David and sits next

to him on settee. David begins to drink and Jessica continues her knitting)

JESSICA: What *did* you tell him, David. What did you tell Peter about me.

DAVID: Nothing, until he asked. Then, we told him his parents had died in India.

JESSICA: Nothing more.

DAVID: Nothing more.

JESSICA: And he was satisfied with only that.

DAVID: Children accept simple explanations.

JESSICA: You became his parents . . . and I was casually dismissed as a death in India.

DAVID: You do not understand children.

JESSICA: That is true, David. There were no children in that prison. Mothers, yes, but no children. *(Pause)* Peter takes more after me than his father, don't you think?

(Neither David nor Freda answers)

JESSICA: Or have I changed so that it is hard to detect any resemblance. Freda and I could almost pass for twins as children but not now . . . not now . . . But then, we have led slightly different lives these past fifteen years. Isn't that true, Freda.

(Freda nods)

JESSICA: Have I changed greatly, Freda? Were you shocked to see how I had changed.

DAVID: *(Softly)* It is always a surprise to see anyone after a long period of time.

JESSICA: Yes, it was a long time. It really wasn't sisterly for me to remain away for so long, was it, Freda.

(Freda looks down at her hands)

JESSICA: And during that long period, Peter never questioned further? Only accepted?

DAVID: Life goes on, Jessica. There must be acceptance, not only by children, but by all of us.

JESSICA: Peter, my son Peter, will he return, do you think?

(There is a pause. David glances at his watch, then quickly puts his cup on table and rises)

DAVID: McLeash will have given me up for lost if I don't get down.

FREDA: You won't be gone long, will you, David.

DAVID: Couple hours, that's all.

(David crosses to doorway right. Freda has risen and gone behind settee)

DAVID: *(At doorway)* You'll be all right, won't you. *(After-thought)* I mean, the both of you.

FREDA: *(Half-heartedly)* Yes, David. But don't be long.

(David looks at both Freda and Jessica and then leaves soberly. Freda takes his cup and returns it to the tea tray at rear of room. She turns slowly toward Jessica)

JESSICA: David has changed very little these last fifteen years. You have changed, Freda. Greatly.

(Jessica continues her knitting. Freda returns slowly to the settee and sits. After a moment she leans forward to Jessica)

FREDA: *(Softly)* Please, Jessica, return the address book.

(Jessica only smiles, but then stops her knitting)

JESSICA: Your begging this way, Freda, reminds me of when we were children at school. You had lost something, very carelessly, which I had found—a locket, I believe. Then, like now, you begged me for it. Do you remember, Freda?

FREDA: *(In pain)* I remember.

JESSICA: I tormented you for several moments—and then do you recall what I did?

FREDA: *(Weakly)* You gave the locket back to me.

(Jessica smiles, then a moment later takes an address book out of her pocket and hands it out to Freda. Freda almost leaps from her position, takes the book, and sinks back onto the settee and begins to cry. Jessica continues her knitting as she watches Freda)

JESSICA: *(Looking out rather than at Freda)* I cried that first night in prison. Only that first night. *Never again.* It was late when they took me into the cell. There were two beds. In one lay a woman I presumed to be sleeping. I could not

28

see her face. After the guards left, I began to weep, burying my face in the pillow, so as not to waken my cellmate. I must have wept for hours before finally falling asleep. When I awoke in the morning, I turned to look at my cellmate. But she was not in her bed. Instead, she was hanging by her neck from the light cord.

(*Freda gasps*)

JESSICA: Her face was terribly distorted and almost purplish from the strangulation.

FREDA: (*Weakly*) Please, Jessica.

JESSICA: But I never cried in that prison again. After that first night I never cried again. (*Pause*) It is remarkable how a human being adjusts to new situations. After a few weeks it seemed as if the prison routine had always been my life. The pattern was hypnotic. Soon there seemed to have been no past —no assurance of any future. Only the present—the routine— the pattern. The clanging of the bells in the morning after a night of fitful sleep. The unlocking of the cells; the standing in front of the cell; the orders screamed out over the sound system; the formation of the line; the marching along the cell corridor, down the iron stairs; into the eating room; the line for the food; waiting for the order to sit at the table; the tinware; the monotonous dreary food; lining up again and marching to our work departments; the work; then the bells clanging; and the lunch period; and marching back to the work area; and again after work the clanging of the bells; and marching to the dining area; then the marching back to the cells; there to wait for sleep to provide escape. (*Pause*) You know, Freda, I never learned the name of that woman who was hanging there above me that first morning in prison.

FREDA: (*Softly*) Poor Jessica.

JESSICA: (*Repeating*) *Poor Jessica.* Each woman had her little dream, her little straw she clutched to retain her reason. Mine was this dream, Freda; to return to my child, to make up all those lost years, to start a new life. If I had known what was to happen, I could not have clutched to that straw; I would not have fought to retain my reason; I would have let myself go under, be taken away to the asylum from which few return . . . Peter, my little boy Peter lost to me. Those years lost . . . lost, lost, Freda, and all because of you . . . You, Freda. I have not deserved this. (*Rising*) You, you, Freda, have deserved this, not I! While I rotted in prison, you went on with your fine husband, your fine home, your fine social position, and with my fine son, while I rotted in that prison. But that is over, Freda. My dear sister, that is all over!

FREDA: (*Terrified*) What are you planning to do, Jessica?
(*Jessica looks at Freda, smiles, then slowly resumes her seat and looks coldly at Freda*)

FREDA: Tell me, Jessica, what are you planning to do?
(*Jessica looks at Freda with a cold smile*)

FREDA: That smile. I remember it from when we were girls. Whenever someone had hurt you, you didn't cry. Instead that smile. What are you planning to do?

JESSICA: (*Softly*) I shall bring that retribution which God has failed to bring. I am the mother of Peter, *not you*. I should have been with him all those years, *not you. I, not you.* (*Pause*) All during the horrible business of the trial and those fifteen years in prison I fought for my sanity—now you are to have a taste of it. Now it is your turn to fight. To fight for your reason, your sanity.

FREDA: I am not strong, Jessica. You might drive me to kill you.

JESSICA: (*Drops knitting*) Oh, Freda, if you would. If you could. That would be the answer. But you are weak. At this moment I long for death at someone else's hands. But also I long for life. I long for the years I've missed. For the son I've lost. You are the straw, Freda, you are the straw here in my new freedom that will save me, save my reason. Only when there has been retribution, may I be reborn, be saved.

FREDA: (*Mumbling*) It can only be a dream, a terribly bad dream.

JESSICA: (*Quickly*) A nightmare, Freda! But will it last fifteen long years. Will it, Freda. Will it last fifteen long years. (*Freda throws her face into her hands, but does not cry. Jessica gets slowly up and walks over near the piano*)

JESSICA: That is the way I remember you at the trial. Head in hands, but not crying. Day after day. And when I was finally put on the stand and questioned about the murder, I thought, this is when Freda will come forward. Freda, my little sister Freda, will come forward with the truth. With the truth that will save me. (*Jessica comes and stands behind the large chair down left and looks at Freda*)

JESSICA: Freda.

(*Freda looks up slowly at Jessica*)

JESSICA: Why *didn't* you come forward . . . and tell the Court, tell the world the truth—what really happened.

FREDA: I wanted to, Jessica! I planned to. But when the moment came, I couldn't. I tried to get out of my seat to come forward, but I couldn't. I couldn't move. And then it was all too late. You were sentenced. It was too late for me then to speak. To save you. (*Looking out*) I had it all planned, Jessica, what I was to say. If I felt there was no other way of saving you, I was to come forward, to interrupt the proceedings. Your Honor, I would say, I must interrupt the Court because before sentence is passed I must be heard. My sister Jessica shot and killed her husband because she found the two of us making love together. (*Long pause*) Your Honor, there was no premeditation; it was committed in a moment of passion with a hunting gun left in the room.

(*After a moment Jessica comes around and sits in the chair and resumes her knitting*)

JESSICA: I couldn't believe it. The sentence. If it weren't for Peter, I would have screamed out the story. I knew you and David would take him, protect him, keep him until my return. The great return. Mother and son. Mother and Peter. Now that is gone. Now all is gone. My only hope—my only salvation—lies in retribution. Your punishment for my total loss.

(Freda pulls herself up slowly and walks behind the settee, grasping it for strength)

FREDA: Ever since we were girls, Jessica, you've always got your way over me. If you are planning to drive me mad, then I know you shall succeed. *(Pause)* While you were away in prison, do you think it was easy for me? Lying awake night after night, wracked with the pangs of guilt. If I had loved your husband or if he had loved me, there might have been some meaning to it all. But it was nothing. A foolish momentary physical attraction. Something afterwards to be considered silly and immediately forgotten. You were in prison. I had your son to raise. Believe me, Jessica, every thought during those fifteen years has been how to do justice to you through Peter. He is a fine boy, Jessica. He has a lovely girl from a good family. And he'll come back, Jessica. You'll be with him again . . . you will be reunited.

(Jessica drops her knitting and clasps her hands. This is her consuming desire)

FREDA: I know Jessica that you have the power to do any thing you want. If your desire is to destroy me, then I shall be destroyed. But if you destroy me, then you also destroy your son. Is that what you desire, Jessica, to also destroy Peter?

(Freda comes around and sits on settee)

FREDA: You have forced me to invite Lady Devenish. You have not told me why but I have guessed. She is the most powerful woman in the area. She is giving a dinner party Saturday before the Ball to which only the most distinguished will be invited. This I know you know. You have said that you desire Peter and a career. At designing. You have lost Peter, but perhaps only momentarily. He will surely return. There is still the other. Use me, Jessica. Use me in any way you wish. David's position is high and secure. Use me, Jessica, use me, but *(pleading)* do not destroy me.

(There is the sound of the doorbell)

JESSICA: Lady Devenish!

(Jessica rises)

JESSICA: Give me a few moments' time. Tell her nothing of me, but confirm all that I say.

(Jessica goes up stairway left. Freda braces herself and goes to doorway entrance right. After a moment she re-enters with LADY DEVENISH, a very dominant middle-aged woman of high breeding. She is followed by LORD DEVENISH, a meek, mousey man wearing knickers and carrying a cap)

LADY DEVENISH: Freda, my dear, I have never known you to act so strangely. It just isn't like a wife of a medical professor to have these mysterious visitors.

FREDA: Tea, Lady Devenish?

LADY DEVENISH: Thank you. *(To Lord Devenish)* Sit there, Herbert. *(Lady Devendish has indicated the piano bench)*

(Lady Devenish crosses over and sits on the settee. Freda brings forward a tea set which she places on the table, takes off cosey, and begins to pour tea)

LADY DEVENISH: Come, dear Freda, do tell me. Is she here?

FREDA: One lump or two?

LADY DEVENISH: One, please. *(Looking toward Lord Devenish)* Tea, Herbert.

(Lord Devenish nods. Lady Devenish then turns back to Freda)

LADY DEVENISH: Most women when they telephone seem to want to talk and gossip for hours. But all I get out of you is that it's necessary I be here at three to meet your guest. *(Turning to Lord Devenish)* Tea, Herbert?

(Again Lord Devenish nods meekly. He sits squarely toward audience at piano bench)

LADY DEVENISH: *(To Freda)* Is she someone famous? Nowadays one may allow for any breach of conduct or morality if there is requisite fame. It seems to have replaced family and breeding as the card of entreé. Tell me, Freda, is she famous.

FREDA: Not exactly.

LADY DEVENISH: Then is she charming? The slightest amount of charm is a delight when in a man, but charm in a woman is only bearable when there is great charm. Tell me, Freda, is she charming?

FREDA: When I knew her before . . . (*Faltering and remembering*) Yes . . . before . . . great charm.

LADY DEVENISH: And now? Perhaps now the substitution of marriage brilliantly contrived or wealth vulgarly displayed?

FREDA: Are your committees going well, Lady Devenish. The Ball committees.

LADY DEVENISH: My committees always go well, dear Freda, because I understand perfectly the principles of delegation and subordination. (*Turning toward Lord Devenish*) Tea, Herbert?

> (*Lord Devenish shakes his head this time in the negative. Lady Devenish gets up mechanically and takes tea to Lord Devenish who takes it politely. Lady Devenish then crosses back toward Freda*)

LADY DEVENISH: My only problem a personal one. My gown—I am so dissatisfied with it. It's very similar to my last ball gown.

FREDA: The one they photographed for *Vogue?*

LADY DEVENISH: Yes. Do you remember the neck line?

> (*Freda rises and crosses over to piano. Lord Devenish moves to end of bench away from the women who stand ignoring him*)

FREDA: I have the issue here, I believe.

> (*Freda looks through a stack of magazines and selects one. Lady Devenish crosses, takes magazine, thumbs through it quickly and finds a page*)

LADY DEVENISH: There. My new gown has an even higher neck line. Cut on the same bias though with a larger sweep of the skirt. Sort of a lime green in color.

> (*Both look up to see Jessica enter and stand at top of stairway left. There has been a slight change in her*)

*hair, a much softer arrangement, but a startling change
in her costume. It is a stunning aquagreen linen suit or
whatever will look stunning on actress playing Jessica.
At railing, Jessica looks toward the two women, displays
a warm radiant smile and comes beautifully down the
stairs and across the room toward the women. Freda, of
course, is shocked, but Lady Devenish does not notice)*

JESSICA: *(Beautifully-voiced)* Lady Devenish. How good
of you to come. And upon such an informal invitation.

*(It is obvious that Lady Devenish is favorably impressed.
Lord Devenish rises to his feet and stands facing Jessica
politely, his cap clutched between his hands. Without
looking at Lord Devenish, Lady Devenish gestures
slightly towards him)*

LADY DEVENISH: *(Matter-of-factly)* Lord Devenish.

*(Jessica is about to say something to Lord Devenish
when Lady Devenish continues speaking)*

LADY DEVENISH: You are, of course, Freda's mysterious
visitor.

JESSICA: I am Carla Morgan. Which, I hasten to add, is
not my true name.

*(Lady Devenish is a little bewildered. Freda nods toward
tea table)*

FREDA: *Carla,* we are having tea. I shall pour you a cup.

*(Freda sits on settee and Lady Devenish joins her.
Jessica sits in large chair facing them)*

JESSICA: Freda and I were in school together. As children.

LADY DEVENISH: Really. *(Noticing Lord Devenish)* Sit
down, Herbert.

(Lord Devenish resumes his seat on the piano bench)

JESSICA: But this is the first time we've been together in
fifteen years.

LADY DEVENISH: Oh, how charming.

JESSICA: I've always thought of Freda as being the one
closest to me. The one to turn to if I ever needed help.

LADY DEVENISH: No one has a more kind, understanding, generous heart than Freda Brooks.

JESSICA: Yes and because of that, I have been most concerned about my presence here. There will be the curious . . . the gossips. (*Pause*) I am using an assumed name, Lady Devenish. I am a widow. I met my husband on the Riviera. Freda knew him well. Freda was at my wedding, a bridesmaid.

(*Lady Devenish looks at Freda who nods weakly*)

JESSICA: (*Rises and stands near chair*) My husband was an Eastern European. It was only because I loved him so that I consented to return with him there. Oh, Lady Devenish, where I lived was truly a prison. For fifteen long years. I loved my husband but the constant fear! My only contact with friends here through smuggled letters. But I loved my husband. One day he was shot. There was no longer any reason to remain in that prison. So now I am here. To pick up my life again. To use a new name by necessity.

LADY DEVENISH: And you have come to Freda.

JESSICA: (*Simply*) I have come to Freda.

LADY DEVENISH: (*Directly*) How may I help you, my dear?

JESSICA: (*Pointing*) That copy of *Vogue*. May I have it?

(*Lady Devenish hands the copy to Jessica*)

JESSICA: I am a designer, Lady Devenish. For the past six years my designs have been smuggled out and used by other designers. (*Thumbing a page*) Do you see this group. Two of these six are mine. But now I am free they shall be mine in name as well as in fact.

(*Lady Devenish examines group*)

LADY DEVENISH: All six are magnificent.

(*Lady Devenish turns several pages and shows Jessica a photo*)

LADY DEVENISH: My new ball gown is similar to this, only with a higher neck line.

JESSICA: (*Looking at picture and then at Lady Devenish*) But this is wrong for you, Lady Devenish. The lines, I mean.

If the neck were lower, perhaps, or a small fold used. To accentuate your beautiful throat. In a Belgium linen, blue tint, you would be magnificent.

LADY DEVENISH: In blue?

JESSICA: A crystal blue. (*Noticing glass held in Act I is on table*) This blue. (*Picks up and holds to light*) In linen it would be shimmering. As this blue crystal is shimmering.

LADY DEVENISH: (*Poignantly*) At the ball I should most like to be shimmering. (*After a moment*) Miss Morgan, will you do my gown for Saturday?

JESSICA: I will try.

LADY DEVENISH: I am having a small dinner before the ball to which you are invited.

JESSICA: Thank you.

LADY DEVENISH: And as for gossip, I shall see that any is quickly stopped.

JESSICA: (*Graciously*) You are very kind.

LADY DEVENISH: (*Concerned*) But could you possibly have the gown by Saturday?

JESSICA: There would be the first sketches. Then we'd need to find the fabric.

LADY DEVENISH: I'll send Herbert over with the car tomorrow about tennish.

(*Jessica nods assent*)

LADY DEVENISH: And you'll have the sketches then, I hope. Perhaps, my dear, you should begin sketching now while I'm still fresh in your mind.

JESSICA: Yes, I should like to go now to begin the sketching.

LADY DEVENISH: Splendid!

(*Jessica crosses over and up the stairway. Lord Devenish rises. He bows to Jessica; she nods to him and to the ladies and exits. Lord Devenish resumes his seat. Lady Devenish crosses over right behind large chair*)

LADY DEVENISH: Oh, Freda, I am indeed grateful to you. I have an uncanny instinct for people. I knew when I entered your visitor was to be someone special. And indeed just what

I need for the dinner. I hope that Miss Morgan will manage to remain unfamiliar so that I might entertain her often. Over-familiarity is a social error that is fatal. Miss Morgan has charm and mystery in exactly the proper proportions. I've an extra man, Lord Bracton, I'll place Miss Morgan next to him.

FREDA: (*Rather weakly*) In textiles, isn't he?

LADY DEVENISH: (*Nodding*) London, but coming up for the ball. A handsome widower whose lechery, I confess, is not from instinct, but rather from habit. A most charming man.

(*Lady Devenish goes over to mirror on right wall near doorway. She opens her collar a bit*)

LADY DEVENISH: You know I do have a lovely throat. (*To Herbert*) Herbert, you've never once mentioned that I had a lovely throat.

(*Herbert begins to speak, but Lady Devenish turns again to admire herself in mirror and to continue speaking*)

LADY DEVENISH: It's funny I never noticed before.

(*Lady Devenish looks at herself back and forth in the mirror. She then glances at her watch*)

LADY DEVENISH: Freda dear, I must run, but I thank you again for inviting me over. I shall see you at the ball. And, of course, at the dinner. And do, Freda, try to have something happen to you or David before then. To whisper about. One should invite to dinner only those who are being whispered about . . . the surest guarantee of party success. Carla Morgan! Yes, Freda, you are indeed fortunate to know such a charming person.

(*Lady Devenish crosses over and shakes hand of Freda*)

LADY DEVENISH: Belgium linen. Blue tint. I'd best begin searching right away. I could, of course, have Lord Bracton send up a piece by air from London. (*Muttering*) Most charming, Miss Morgan, most charming. (*Goes to doorway*)

FREDA: I'll see you out.

(*Freda goes to doorway. Lady Devenish turns toward Herbert*)

LADY DEVENISH: Come, Herbert!
(*Lord Devenish rises, bows to Freda, and follows Lady Devenish who is followed by Freda. A moment later, Jessica reenters. Her hair is severe again and she is wearing her gray prison dress. She carries her knitting. She walks across to large chair down left, sits, and begins knitting. Freda reenters and sees Jessica*)
JESSICA: (*In cold metallic voice and without looking at Freda*) The clanging of the bells in the morning after a night of fitful sleep.
(*Freda starts slowly toward French windows as if an animal trapped*)
JESSICA: The unlocking of the cells; the standing in front of the cell; the orders screamed out over the sound system; the formation of the line; the marching along the cell corridor, down the iron stairs; into the eating room; the line for the food; waiting for the order to sit at the table; the tinware; the monotonous dreary food; lining up again and marching to our work departments; the work; then the bells clanging; and the lunch period; and marching back to the work area; and again after work the clanging of the bells; and marching to the dining area; then the marching back to the cells; there to wait for sleep to provide escape.
(*The curtains have slowly closed during above speech*)

END OF ACT II

TIGER IN CRYSTAL

ACT III

(As the scene opens David is sitting in the large chair down left, seemingly reading his newspaper, but glancing with concern at Freda, who sits on the settee, busying herself with the tea things.)

FREDA: I'll have your tea in a moment, David.

(Freda picks up empty cup and saucer and is about to reach for the teapot when the empty cup and saucer fall from her hand with a crash. Freda throws herself back in the settee and buries her face in her hands. David puts his paper in his lap and looks at Freda with concern. After a moment Freda looks up at David. It is obvious from her physical condition and voice that she is in an advanced state of nervous exhaustion)

FREDA: I'm sorry, David. It's just that . . . I don't know if I can go on much longer . . . Somehow I managed to live with the past, but I can't live with the present. It is too, too terrible.

DAVID: Please, Freda.

FREDA: How easy it must be for one to go mad. Just the worry about Peter is enough . . . Why haven't we heard? No word at all. Not knowing where he is . . . whether he's alive or dead. Whether we'll ever see him again.

DAVID: Peter's all right, Freda. Now don't worry.

FREDA: How do you know?

DAVID: I just know.

FREDA: You've received word?

DAVID: No, but in my heart I'm certain he's all right.

FREDA: I keep walking into his room. That empty room. Empty but still so full of Peter. Perhaps we should have told him . . . before . . . when he was old enough . . . then maybe this would not have happened. Perhaps we should have prepared him for Jessica.

(*At the mention of the word a tremble sweeps over Freda*)

FREDA: Poor Jessica . . . all those years . . . and then to lose her son.

DAVID: Things will work themselves out.

FREDA: When, David, when? Jessica is not well. She thinks she built a shell against those prison experiences. But the shell was not strong enough. Those fifteen years in prison did do something to her. Did leave Jessica a little mad. And now the shock of Peter. Something must be done, David. I can't go on. I am consumed more and more by my pity, by my anguish. It is possible, David, that like Jessica, I shall also become a little mad.

(*Freda again buries herself in her hands and cries audibly. David rises, goes to her, and comforts her*)

FREDA: (*Looking up*) All over the city there are couples like us, having tea together. Husbands and wives having quiet cups of tea. The wives asking if the day had gone well and the husbands asking the same. All over the city. But not here. Not here. Perhaps never again those quiet cups of tea and those polite questions. Perhaps only whispered questions such as Where in the world might our son be? Or, how long is fifteen years when spent in a prison?

DAVID: Freda, don't torment yourself this way.

FREDA: Torment? Oh, David, if it were *only* torment.

DAVID: We'll have those quiet cups of tea and those quiet little conversations again. (*Rising*) And I'll go back to hitting the wrong notes in Haydn. (*Crosses to piano. He sits and plays for a few moments and conspicuously hits a wrong note*)

FREDA: (*Smiling*) Oh, David, you did that on purpose.

(*David beckons Freda over. She sits beside him as he plays. She leans against him and is happy for a moment. The doorbell rings. Freda rises quickly and goes over to stand behind settee facing doorway right. She again*) *is tense. David exits through doorway right and soon reenters with Sally and George. They are in sober contrast to Act I)*

SALLY: Good morning, Dr. Brooks . . . Mrs. Brooks.

(Freda steps toward Sally)

FREDA: Have you seen him. Have you seen Peter?

SALLY: Yes.

FREDA: And is he all right? Safe?

GEORGE: Peter is all right.

FREDA: *(Sinking onto sette)* Thank God. Thank God. My boy is safe. Where is he? Where is our boy?

(Sally notices the tea things)

DAVID: Would you like some tea, children?

SALLY: Thank you, yes.

GEORGE: I can't stay. Train leaves in two hours.

FREDA: To the University?

GEORGE: Yes, and I'm not half-finished with packing.

FREDA: *(To George)* Will Peter be with you on that train?

GEORGE: *(After pause)* I don't know, Mrs. Brooks. I don't think so.

FREDA: And you, Sally?

SALLY: Father has wired I'll be late in beginning classes.

GEORGE: It won't be the same—going back without Peter. *(Turning)* Dr. Brooks, could you see that Sally gets home.

DAVID: Of course.

(George goes slowly toward the door)

GEORGE: It's funny how life suddenly can just go to pieces. Like that. *(Snaps finger seriously)*

(George turns soberly and starts out. David puts his arms around his shoulder and accompanies him out of room. Freda sits on settee, picks up pot, and feels it)

FREDA: Oh, the tea is cold.

SALLY: Never mind, Mrs. Brooks.

(Freda picks up pot and starts off exit left)

FREDA: It'll only take me a moment. *(Turning)* Peter does not want us to know his whereabouts?

43

SALLY: No. But he sends his love . . . to you both.

FREDA: Bless you, my dear, bless you for coming.

(*Freda exits. Sally walks slowly over and sits in large chair down right. David reenters*)

SALLY: Mrs. Brooks has gone for tea.

(*David nods and then crosses over slowly and sits on settee. Both are quiet for a moment*)

SALLY: (*Softly*) Peter is staying at a little country inn.

DAVID: (*Anxiously*) He is safe. Our boy is safe.

SALLY: Yes. (*Pause*) Peter has told me very little. Only that he had discovered his mother is alive and had been in prison. Is that true, Dr. Brooks?

DAVID: Yes, it is true.

SALLY: Poor Peter.

DAVID: Will that make any difference between you?

SALLY: Why should it? I've talked with Father and Father's only concern is that Peter might not return to the University because of this . . . It was strange talking with father. And yet so easy. It's the first time we've ever worked out a problem together . . . Talking with him was not like talking to my father at all, but to someone I had known—not very well—and someone I would want to know better . . . It is strange, but I think father and I became friends . . . last night . . . for the first time. There's been a change. I'm not his little girl any more . . . and I'm glad. Last night during our talk I became a woman and father became a friend who was helping me . . . Can you understand, Dr. Brooks, can you possibly understand.

DAVID: I understand, Sally. I understand.

(*Freda reenters carrying pot of tea. She crosses over to settee*)

FREDA: There now, we'll all have a hot cup of tea.

(*Freda sits down and pours tea. In the midst of filling one cup, she holds pot in air and looks out*)

FREDA: (*Cheerfully*) How could we possibly get along without afternoon tea? Those lovely moments forcing us to

44

pause . . . and to reflect . . . and to be sociable. There you are, my dear.

(*Freda hands cup to Sally and one to George. They all settle back and drink*)

FREDA: It is, I suppose, a ritual—tea drinking. I think if it is ever given up, a little part of civilizing will also be given up. (*Almost play-acting at normalcy*) I have noticed an increased crispness in the air as of late. Summer will soon be over and autumn will be with us. Have you noticed?

DAVID: Yes, just in the last few days.

FREDA: (*Play-acting at normalcy*) It will soon be time to dig up the bulbs. Put them away for winter. I love autumn best. Sally, which is your favorite season?

SALLY: Spring.

FREDA: When I was a girl, spring was also my favorite. But now I am older. Old, perhaps. Autumn is my favorite. I suppose spring is favored by most because it signifies rebirth, a renewal of earth's promises. (*In drifting voice*) But, in a way, autumn is also a promise. (*Softly*) Not of death, but of life. A different sort of life perhaps. Autumn, winter, spring, summer. And then autumn again. (*Pause*) For some.

(*Freda stares out almost blankly in front of her. There is a long pause. Sally puts down her cup and rises*)

SALLY: I'm sorry, Mrs. Brooks, but I must leave.

FREDA: (*Recovering*) Oh, you can't stay a bit longer? I do so enjoy your company.

SALLY: I'm sorry.

DAVID: I'll run you home. It'll only take a moment.

(*Sally shakes hands with Freda. Then she goes to doorway right and turns to Freda*)

FREDA: (*Play-acting at normalcy*) Thank you so much, my dear, for coming to tea.

(*Just as Sally is about to exit, Jessica appears on the stair landing. She wears her gray dress. Both Sally and David turn to look at her. Freda looks at her, then turns her head toward David and Sally*)

SALLY: (*Stepping forward*) You are Jessica.

JESSICA: Yes, I am Jessica.

SALLY: I am Sally—a friend of Peter's.

(Jessica stands without speaking. After a moment David turns toward Jessica)

DAVID: I'm driving Sally home. You'll no doubt meet again.

(Jessica continues to stand without comment. David turns to escort Sally from the room. Freda steps forward)

FREDA: (*Anxiously*) David!

DAVID: Yes, Freda.

FREDA: You won't be gone long.

DAVID: Be right back.

(David looks anxiously from Freda to Jessica and then back to Freda and quickly follows Sally. Jessica pauses a moment more and then comes down the steps and over to the piano area. Freda still continues to stand near the settee)

JESSICA: The dinner was a triumph, Freda. It was too bad you became ill and could not attend.

FREDA: I wanted to, Jessica. I wanted to see you the way you were when we were girls. Beautifully gowned, sparkling in the candlelight. Charming all you met. But I kept vomiting. Again and again. All evening. That is the truth, Jessica.

JESSICA: I am sorry that you were ill, Freda. Truly sorry.

FREDA: At the dinner, at the ball, Jessica, did you get what you wanted?

JESSICA: Yes, Freda, I got what I wanted. Some things in life are so easy to obtain. (*Leans against piano with arms spread on each side*) Last night was one of the great moments in my life. One of those moments signifying change. Great change. It is rare when a person can point to an exact moment when his life is significantly changed. I have had those moments. (*Pause*) Mother's death and being sent to school in the Alps . . . That night I found you and George together . . . That court statement pronouncing me guilty. Peter's rejection. Last night's dinner . . .

Lady Devenish was brilliant. Her gown surpassed all others. Last night saw the birth of a new career. Carla Morgan, designer.

FREDA: I am glad for you, Jessica.

JESSICA: Half of my dream—only half. The other half, reunion with Peter. Mother and son. My boy Peter who is lost to me.

FREDA: What are your plans, Jessica?

JESSICA: I shall continue to live here, Freda.

FREDA: Here?

JESSICA: Yes.

FREDA: For how long, Jessica?

JESSICA: How long? Perhaps forever.

FREDA: Forever.

(*Freda sinks onto settee as she utters above words. Jessica crosses and stands behind large chair*)

JESSICA: I am not well, Freda. I thought I had built such a strong wall inside that I would not be hurt by prison. But I was hurt—terribly. This I now realize. I left that prison with unnatural sensations which may be a kind of madness. The lines, the forms, the colors, the crystal. That tiger in crystal, Freda. I sometimes think that is what I am becoming. That tiger in crystal. It is a dreadful sickness, Freda. But it was that sickness which created Lady Devenish's gown. Perhaps such brilliance can only come from the very sick. And in with these forms and lines and colors, there is Peter who is my son. Also there is you, Freda, mixed in with it all. I seem to be hopelessly enmeshed. To be well again I must bring all under control— the lines, the forms, the colors, the crystal. That tiger must stalk no longer. To be well again you must play a part—a significant part.

FREDA: Let me help you, Jessica.

JESSICA: (*Coming from behind chair*) I love you, Freda. You are all I have now. Mother gone. Father gone. Just the two of us. Along together, as when we were children. Do you remember when we first set off on that long train trip to boarding school after mother's death. Alone, frightened, all, all alone. As if we were the only two in the world. Having only each other. Do you remember, Freda.

FREDA: I remember.

JESSICA: And we swore to love and help one another as long as both should live.

FREDA: I remember.

JESSICA: Oh, Freda, if we could only go back. Be girls again. Sisters, hand-in-hand. If only we could have remained those two little girls. Hand-in-hand. Never grown up . . . If only we could have remained together—as sisters—as friends. Long ago. Hand-in-hand. Long ago. Long, long ago . . . Now, this illness, this dreadful illness. From which I must be saved. I must be saved. You, you Freda, only you can save me.

FREDA: How? How, Jessica, how?

JESSICA: Only you can save me, Freda.

FREDA: How, Jessica?

(*Long pause*)

JESSICA: Do you truly wish to help me, Freda?

FREDA: Yes, truly.

JESSICA: You wish to help me because I am your sister. The only one left to you of our family. You wish to help me because of our childhood oath.

FREDA: Yes, Jessica.

JESSICA: And you wish to help me because you know it is you who have caused my illness.

FREDA: Yes, Jessica, it is I who am responsible.

JESSICA: To save me, you must be brave, Freda, courageous. You must take my hand as when we were children. You must come with me into the unknown, leave all behind; sacrifice all for my salvation.

FREDA: What am I to do, Jessica?

(*Jessica crosses over to Freda and stands over her*)

JESSICA: Help bring God's retribution. Cleanse your guilt. You must take my hand. You must come with me. Come with me into this world in which I have fallen.

FREDA: No!

JESSICA: This has been my punishment, but I have not deserved it. You have deserved it. You have deserved it, Freda, not I.

FREDA: No, Jessica!

JESSICA: You must come with me into this world, be punished as I am being punished; join me in this Hell to cleanse yourself of guilt.

(Freda stands and turns to go. Jessica grabs her)

JESSICA: This is the only way, Freda.

FREDA: No, Jessica.

JESSICA: You must. To be cleansed. Yes, Freda, then the two of us will work our way back together. Hand-in-hand as when we were children long ago in the Alps. Hand-in-hand. This is the only way, Freda. The only salvation for us both. Don't fight, Freda.

FREDA: *(Weakly)* I must fight.

JESSICA: Slip away. Slip away, Freda. Come with me, to that world of form and line and color. Escape. Leave all behind. Escape. Come slip away, Freda. Slip away.

(Freda screams and runs from Jessica)

FREDA: Don't, Jessica. For God's sake, don't. I *am* slipping. Someone save me.

(Freda falls onto knees grasping arm of the large chair. David enters. He looks at Jessica who is standing near the settee and looks at David)

DAVID: *(Softly)* Go to your room, Freda.

(Freda has stopped her hysterical sobbing. David slowly helps her to her feet and escorts her up stairway. Freda avoids looking at Jessica as she crosses to stairway. Jessica remains motionless, staring out during previous action. David crosses to area down right slowly and then turns toward Jessica)

DAVID: *(Softly)* Jessica, I want you to leave this house.

(Jessica shows no notice of David. David goes to closet upstage right and takes out black trenchcoat and large

49

purse. He carries these down and places them on piano bench. He turns again to Jessica)

DAVID: I have had pity for you, Jessica. I have waited and watched while you adjusted to this life which is new for you. You have perhaps thought me weak, because I have not interrupted. It was not weakness, Jessica, but compassion. Compassion because you were not reunited with your son. But there is an end to pity. An end to compassion. I shall find a place for you somewhere. Take care of the expense. You are never to see my wife again.

JESSICA: *(Simply)* Freda is my sister.

DAVID: In that other life, perhaps. *(Crossing toward Jessica)* You are a very sick woman, Jessica. You need help.

JESSICA: You are a doctor, David.

DAVID: I am not blind, Jessica. I have seen your effect upon Freda. I hoped that something would happen to change this terrible course. You have turned Freda into a desperate woman.

JESSICA: For fifteen years I knew only desperate women. And when I looked into a mirror, that is what I saw. A desperate woman.

DAVID: If you continue, I shudder at the consequences.

JESSICA: Will she murder me, do you think?

DAVID: Would you like that, Jessica?

(Jessica thinks, but expresses no answer)

DAVID: I'll call for a taxi. I do this only because of my anxiety for Freda and for you. You're to stay in a hotel until I've made arrangements.

JESSICA: I must remain here, David. I must be here . . . when my son returns . . . The home of my son. The home of my sister Freda.

DAVID: You are driving Freda mad.

JESSICA: So soon. It took that prison fifteen years.

(David crosses to telephone which is on table near the bar table upstage right)

JESSICA: Don't telephone, David. (*Commanding and pointing to chair*) Sit here. I have something I must say.

(*David replaces the phone in its cradle and crosses over and sits in large chair down left*)

JESSICA: I find your concern for Freda most commendable. If only Freda had shown me the same concern. If only you would show me the same concern.

DAVID: I am concerned about you, Jessica. My every thought, every action is for your personal welfare.

JESSICA: Those prison years can only be erased, the loss of my son can only be erased, David, by seeing the punishment of the one really responsible. Freda! (*Angrily*) There, I have said it! I shall remain here, David, because it is necessary for my salvation and because when I have told you my story you will not want, will not dare have me leave.

DAVID: If you won't go into a nursing home, Jessica, at least go to some place quiet. Away somewhere to forget.

JESSICA: Forget? I do not want to forget. I want to work things out. To arrange; to rearrange. To have my mind clear again; to have it free of hate and guilt and revenge.

DAVID: I am a doctor. I will help you. But not here.

JESSICA: (*Angrily*) Here, David here! This is where I shall see my son again. (*Quietly*) Yes, David, I have something to tell you. (*Rises and circles behind settee and large chair in which David is sitting to downstage right*) Oh yes, David, I have something to tell you . . . at the trial you may remember no motive was established for the murder . . . but there was a motive, David . . . It was a crime of passion. The passion I felt when I found my husband making love to another woman . . . another woman, David, do you understand? And that other woman? Your wife, David. Freda . . . your wife Freda!

(*David is silent*)

JESSICA: (*Stepping forward*) Now it is your turn, David. Take a gun. Go now, David, go to her.

(*David looks at Jessica for a moment and then settles back in the settee*)

51

JESSICA: Go, David, for God's sake go! Why don't you go! (*Sudden realization*) You know! You've known all along! (*Shocked*) And you've permitted her to live!

> (*David looks at Jessica for a moment and then leans forward on the settee*)

DAVID: (*Quietly*) I love my wife. My wife *cares* for me. In every human relationship, Jessica, there is that margin which love brings. The width of the margin is measured by the depth of the love. In that margin there is understanding, compassion, forgiveness. You must seek that margin, Jessica. With me, with Freda, and with Peter. Seek that margin, Jessica. Understand. Forgive.

> (*Jessica starts toward David's chair when suddenly both look toward doorway as Peter enters and stands. David rises quickly*)

DAVID: Peter!

> (*Jessica goes slightly behind chair and grasps it for support*)

PETER: Could I see Jessica. Alone?

> (*David looks at Peter, then at Jessica, then nods and goes up stairway and exits. Peter remain standing near doorway. Jessica crosses and stands behind settee*)

PETER: I came back, Jessica, to ask your forgiveness.

JESSICA: (*Weakly*) Peter.

> (*Peter slowly crosses the room*)

PETER: I want to be your friend, Jessica. I don't know what went wrong with me. Will you forgive me.

JESSICA: (*Weakly*) Forgive?

PETER: I realize now that the love Mum and Dad gave to me was in part the love they felt for you.

JESSICA: Love. For me?

PETER: Yes.

JESSICA: I too gave you love, Peter. All those long years behind prison bars, I gave you love. But you did not know.

You did not know . . . Now, Peter, you shall know. Oh, Peter, you shall know my love for you.

(Jessica wants to go to Peter, but is stopped by his silence and immobile position)

JESSICA: There are so many things we must do—together. We shall make up for all those lost years. Together, Peter, together. Mother and son. This has been my dream, Peter. I've made so many plans. We'll do whatever you wish. Together, Peter.

(Peter remains silent)

JESSICA: If you like I could take a small flat somewhere near the University. Have quiet dinners together, sometimes have your friends over. Summers we could travel abroad. The mountains, the seacoasts, anywhere you like. I don't care, just as long as we're together.

(Peter is still silent)

JESSICA: I realize it will take a little while for us to become reacquainted. *(Pause)* Do you remember anything about me . . . from before?

PETER: *(After a pause)* My earliest memories are of Dad giving up his practice in England to come here. To lecture. Giving up a brilliant career. Now, I know it was for me—for me. And for you. This is our bond, Jessica. Their love for us.

JESSICA: *(Repeating softly)* Jessica. You still cannot call me mother.

(Peter attempts to say something but cannot. Jessica pauses for a very long moment)

JESSICA: What a fine boy you are . . . now straight and strong you stand . . . What a fine boy you are. *(Softly)* David and Freda have done their job well. *(Another long pause and then Jessica puts her hand to her forehead)* How strange it all is. How my head is clearing. The forms, the lines, the colors all fitting into place.

(Jessica crosses around and sits on settee)

JESSICA: Sit down, Peter.

(*Jessica indicates large chair down left. Peter sits*)

JESSICA: You leave tomorrow for the University?

PETER: Yes.

(*There is a long pause. Jessica leans forward a little to Peter, but Peter does not move. Jessica settles back a little in settee. Something seems to be draining from her as she seems to be fighting the making of a decision. She then leans quickly forward*)

JESSICA: Try, Peter, try. Try to call me Mother.

(*Peter struggles, but can say nothing. He drops his head, but does not move otherwise. After a long pause, Jessica slowly rises and goes upstage. After a moment she notices the piece of blue crystal. She picks it up slowly and looks about the room as if for the last time. She does not look toward Peter as she gives her next speech*)

JESSICA: I, too, am leaving, Peter. (*Very softly*) Because of my love for you. (*Bravely*) You see (*Gesturing slightly*) I was about to call a taxi.

PETER: (*Weakly*) Mine is still outside.

JESSICA: (*Turning toward Peter*) I go to London, Peter. Lord Bracton has suggested I open a salon. Lord and Lady Devenish will be sponsors.

PETER: (*Painfully*) Is this what you want, Jessica?

(*Jessica looks at Peter without answering, then turns and crosses over to piano bench right where she picks up coat and purse. Peter rises, but stands where he is*)

JESSICA: You know, Peter, it would be most damaging if London knew I had a grown son. We may meet occasionally at parties. There should be a special recognition, don't you think? I think there should be a special recognition between friends.

PETER: A smile, perhaps.

JESSICA: Yes, a smile. Show me, Peter.
(Peter smiles a little slyly)
JESSICA: And my return smile.
(Jessica also smiles a little slyly. She then turns and leaves the room without looking back at Peter who stands looking after her as curtains slowly close)

END OF PLAY